Soliton

SOLITON

ROALD HOFFMANN

for Peter
some recent poems
Roald
10/7/03

POEMS

Copyright © 2002 Roald Hoffmann

All rights reserved

Printed in the United States of America

New Odyssey Series

Published by Truman State University Press, Kirksville, Missouri 63501

http://tsup.truman.edu

Library of Congress Cataloging-in-Publication Data

Hoffmann, Roald.
   Soliton / by Roald Hoffmann.
      p. cm. — (New odyssey series)
   ISBN 1-931112-19-3 (alk. paper)
   I. Title. II. Series.
   PS3558.03468 S67 2002
   811'.54—dc21

2002151574

Cover art: "Seaward" 1994 (detail) © Charles Seliger; private collection, London; courtesy Michael Rosenfeld Gallery, New York, N.Y.

Cover design: Teresa Wheeler

Printed by: McNaughton & Gunn, Saline, Michigan

Type is set in ITC Legacy Serif

Contents

V

VI

VII

Acknowledgments

Some of the poems in this collection were written in a farmhouse in the midst of vineyards between Lacoste and Bonnieux, in the Luberon, France. Crystal Woodward introduced me to this landscape, and showed me ways to look at it; for this I am grateful to her.

Several poems have been published in periodicals and anthologies; I thank the editors for their confidence in my writing: *Chelsea* ("Natural History"); *Colorado Review* ("Olive Tree Master"); *Connecting Creations: Science-Technology-Literature-Arts* ("Why I Didn't Visit the Camp," "Oligopoem," "The Philosopher's Stone Found in January"); *The Kenyon Review* ("Flat Stones Beg to Be Recycled," "Malacology"); *The Massachusetts Review* ("Dream Corps"); *Michigan Quarterly Review* ("Fields of Vision"); *Midstream* ("In View of the Promised Land"); *Notre Dame Review* ("Tsunami," "Cupping"); *Pembroke Magazine* ("We Will Not Be Moved," "Birdland"); *Rendezvous* ("Isaac's Fall"); *Southern Humanities Review* ("Interface").

I

Tsunami

for Maria Matos

A soliton is
a singularity
of wave
motion, an edge
traveling just
that way. We saw
one, once
filmed moving heed-
lessly cross
a platinum surface.
Solitons pass
through
each
other
unperturbed.

You are a wave.
Not standing, nor
traveling, satisfying
no equation.
You are a wave
which will not be (Fourier)
analyzed.
You are a wave; in
your eyes I sink
willingly.

Not solitons,
we can't pass through
unaltered.

Why I Didn't Visit the Camp

My son gave me
a salamander pin;
he wrote, Pappa, you
like the salamander
have been through fire.

Not I, but another.
Who said, how we burn,
burn, but why do we not
burn with thick smoke,
with a fatter flame?

Today, we measure
mercury round
crematoria; there,
he smiled, we floated
ashes in water
to part the gold.

The memory is frozen
in pockmarked glaze,
viscous flow arrested
in dark drops, black
lined crackles. I do not
need to see the kiln
to know this pot
has been through fire.

Shall You Dance?

No choice; the very
idea makes you reach

for a tension; casts
off collagen's

triple strand, through
ratcheted micro-

motions, into muscle
cells, then tendon ex-

tension, arm arc;
the neck, your

red-brown hair
follow through 'til

the air, waiting
all *tohu vevohu*,

snaps wise to the line.
Afterwards, you say

"You ask me
which muscle hurts;

whatever muscle
I move is the one

that hurts." Still,
when you climb,

in your breath
you hear life pass-

ing out of you;
when you dance,

music hides
the sound. Such

taut carving
of air by body

will start a con-
flagration,

could make time
a semiclassical

approximation.

Dream Corps

In my country if you wake, snatched
from the dream half-done, you ring
the alarm, there's a pull by every bed

(in my country) and soon, their cars
flashing green in the night, friends come,
for they know I would do it for them,

come to help me re-enter the dream.
They build the set—I sit—a bridge,
killing shadows under it, all these

they paint, high steps, a pub. From a truck
they roll out mirrors, chests, dress a boy
in Elizabethan street costume, teach him

to pour ale. In the half-dark my friends
pat each other, practice their lines, and
whisper to me "tell us where to stand,

tell us what to say." "You are the director,"
my friends say. It matters to them
that I dream, that I dream on in my country.

II

Isaac's Fall

1

Abraham our father named
the falls for the boy, who
on their way up the mountain
first heard their hidden waters.
But there was no time to stop,
holy things to be done. Then
Isaac fled into the desert and
Abraham came on them alone.

2

Isaac's fall sets out with a stock-
still green sheet, a hint wavering
its low edge, where jutting rock
astonishingly dry on end, cleaves
the curtain, and then, which is now,
chaos and gravity brawl in hissing
plunge of water breaking up ledge
to obstacle ledge. Abraham's eyes
follow a stream down, then slip
free of that flux, up to where
choice made itself available,
in a notch of white foam, to be
pulled again, in spurts braiding
inexorably down, to the severed
waters' into dear water reunion.
Downstream, in quiet green pools,
over flat rocks, the water rests.

3

Abraham followed a goat track
to the top of the falls, watched
an olive branch float to the rim.
He found it, silver leaves unbroken,
in the pool below. Abraham dreamt
of waters rising in the desert,
turned by God's breath to clouds

and rain, he woke to Isaac's fall's
hiss, heard the song of first things,
of the waterfall whose end is in its
beginning. The orders of creation
denominated, in his power, Abraham
the Magician unhitched his donkey
to ride down the mountain, to tell
Sarah their son would be back, soon.

In View of the Promised Land

This poem owes much to a painting by Timolé, and an essay,
"The Spring and the Bush" by Michel Tournier, in his The Mirror of Ideas.

The night before he died,
Moses our teacher dreamt

of the waters that once split
for him, now washing over

the burning bush on Horeb; Moses
woke, and smiled at his fate,

to lead a kvetching folk
from oasis to water hole; he,

drawn from water, giving
himself to fire, chosen

for expertise in the miracles
of aquifers and desalination!

Moses found it—again and
again—from the bitter waters

of Marah to the wilderness
of Zin; tired, there at Meribah,

he struck the rock twice, did not
speak to it, as was commanded,

as if to say, God, another miracle!
At Meribah Moses gave up

on his people; for this defiance
he would not enter the land

of milk and honey. They
say we do not know where

God buried Moses, having killed
him with a kiss. I know.

In every green mountain that
catches fire, in the yellow-red

night wounds of that fire,
on the day after, in black

that sucks light from the slopes
—there is Moses. The mistral

then comes, and blows the ashes
up in a cloud that exiles

day from the valley. In
the slopes is where Moses lies.

And drinks—rains, phase
of birth.The mountainside

grows green, as it must. And
Moshe *rabbenu* smiles (as

the priests did not let him
in his book), now at peace

with his fire and his water.

Olive Tree Master

The olive tree master veiled his meaning
    on purpose, a matter of Spanish habit, but
      it broke through, like wild poppies.
He said I will go and spend the night
    watching for wolves in the olive groves—
      who would deny him that—and he took
a Toledo blade (or was it Damascene?); there
    were no wolves, but he was cut by words,
      he said later, their sharp two-sidedness. This
sowed disbelief; he was disguised, brown-
    furrowed nature disguised, like him. The Marrano
      dreamt he was swinging on a long rope
over a caldera, caught in cold hope
    of reaching an edge, wondering on every pass
      whose godly hand lay at the fulcrum.

Imitation of the Mothers

Yechiel Mechl, the *maggid* of Złoczów,
was asked by his disciples:
How can we emulate
the mothers: Sarah, Rebecca,
Rachel and Leah, how
could we aspire
to their acts?

He'd send them to see you dance.
First, to the one
who teaches the service of the body
quiescent;
he would ask them to watch
how pity may be held in stillness of neck, and
your arms rise, instructing time
in the ancient gests of holding daughters
and letting sons go.
He would say:
you teach devotion
better than I do, and
rising from his rough table, he
would turn his questioners' eyes to you,
for the offering of fire turned curvilinear, the service
of the body empowered, the fluid
warm arch of your torso prescient
of where the sweep of your arms
might take you. With you,
they could move aquifers,
they could land on Venus.
Caught up, dancing himself, Yechiel Mechl
would bring them before you,
young one. At first tense, uncertain
of your place or sex,
you do the steps they've taught you.
Then someone taps you on the shoulder, that's
love—you put on your shoes, and
on point,

oh on point,
you are you.
What follows? Well—
life's issue, pleating tresses,
your callused farmhouse hands. Someone's
always leaving you, and there, center point,
you stand,
rooted but turning,
like an empty carousel. Yours,
daughter, mother, wife,
is the service,
of life.

Yechiel Mechl, stern master,
still a Chasid,
would tell the fiddler: *Nu,*
start a new tune. Let women dance,
as Miriam did
after the parting of the waters;
let each
in her own way
as it is said, do
what has not yet been done.

Natural History

In Block 18 the professor from Amsterdam
traded his shirt for a stub of a pencil
and a school notebook, ruled in sections

for beating, by implement—rifle butt, hose
or hand; transgressions of the Hippocratic Oath;
making people watch death, by kind of death;

making people steal. Not to remember, he said,
but to learn, the way in 1652 Menasseh
ben Israel listed demons—possessors, imps,

snatchers of purses and cats, poltergeists,
dybbuks, child killers—evil put in order,
like Brazilian vipers, inventoried, soon

understood. Before they took him to the KB
he paid Jean two crusts to guard the book. Who
sold it, page by page, for rolling cigarettes.

Cupping

A quiet fire brought it back, how
at night Dyuk let him into the attic;
and the strong uncle from the forest

(who gave the guns to my father),
my uncle Fromtchie falls, lies sense-
less eight days with a fever; there

being no medicine, just herbs, and
no doctor to be trusted, we're hiding,
my mother asks Dyuk for some glasses,

a spirit lamp; they try to put me to bed,
but I watch as she bares his back
and heats the glasses, two shatter,

and with a face I do not recognize
she puts them on his back, jam jars,
big glasses, he squirms—they burn,

Aunt Nunia puts a gag over his mouth,
the small boy watches in lamp light
the flesh and blood rise; red welts,

and Uncle Fromtchie falls, sweating, asleep.
My mother cried—she held me—it was
the only thing she knew she could do,

and she hurt him. Long after the war
I saw a fine set, gleaming in a wood case
with an Edinburgh label, cups of all sizes—

every one smaller (though I had grown)
than what was given my mother,
And tongs to hold them; she had none,

nor chemists' hands. After the war,
in New York, Fromtchie/Frank ran
a small factory making hard candy,

he let me watch the food color mixed
into molten sugar, sweet spaghettis
extruded from the ovens, spun by hand

like Venetian millefiori, to be cut warm.
I asked him "Aren't you afraid of being
burned?" and he smiled. Then there was

partner trouble, and one night, in a four-
alarm fire, the factory burned. A caramel
fire, I wondered? And where his scars were.

Flat Stones Beg to Be Recycled

We go back, my mother
and I, back to Złoczów,

where Ukrainian girls
in red and black em-

broidery sing a song,
offer us bread and salt,

for we are guests in their
town, aren't we? But

we look down, clement
June turns December,

snow begins to fall,
outline the scratches

in the paving stones
so they grow into

Hebrew letters. We
stand in a minefield.

My mother has trouble
seeing in the snow.

The Reflection

We all have our fears; mine
to stand in front of a window
at night. Back home, waking
for a drink, I turn on the light,
I look out, through myself, into
black. This is how it will end.

It came back to me, in a rush,
the day I headed up a trail
marked with red blazes. I'd
climb the Luberon; a friend
said no, don't go alone; hunters
have the wild boars nervous.

So I went alone, in short order
lost the trail and found a rough
old road instead, a cut settling
into a slope; there were stone
markers—the old high road
from Ménerbes to Bonnieux.

Then there were shots. I stopped
and said: I know it'll be through
a window. Because in forty-three,
in the attic, there was a window
and a six-year-old looked out
it every day. No shots were heard

but there had been, and outside,
out of any safe place, there were...
men. Who shot my father. Who'd
kill the love left in the attic.
But a window was the world,
for inside it was simply dark.

That understood, I ate the last
of my clementines, saw a tree
an aging man could climb
if *sangliers* rushed. The shots
kept coming, but it felt safe; it
was day, it wouldn't happen here.

III

For Every Thing There is a Time

I wouldn't trade it in for any other, this fine rose hip
kind of a world; where orchards and wild thickets

meet, a fruit falls, to be trampled by dogs and boars—
the seed rooting, wild biochemistries engage, antenna

chlorophylls soak up sunlight, propelling a cascade
of energies and intermediates; upscale, the same light

draws painters to Provence, and elsewhere people shine
lasers on plants' intent femtosecond miracles. Meanwhile,

long after insects and people signed the ur-compact
that to both red should matter, the bush flowers

in the many-petaled wild rose's tight seduction of color.
And in ocher Roussillon Beckett hides in 43–45;

to the east we die, oh this century of thorns and roses!
In Ithaca sense is made of 3-D networks of antimonides

and tellurides, euro-ecumenically "The Merry Widow"
is playing in Avignon, ghosts of popes and William

of Ockham in attendance. And in Bonnieux the fruit
ripens, holding to withered flower, like poem to love;

the hips' form, unthrown Japanese vases; the fruit
is soft to firm, dried for hot tea with hibiscus,

or a Swedish *nyponsoppa*, inside the hairy pip a girl
once put down my shirt. This time, the world soars,

sweet world, allowing the hip rose to define orange red.

Raisins for Being

They left small bunches
on the vine, green late-
comers; the farmers

knew the day to pick,
sugar rising in the
berries, rain offshore. But

four sunny days broke
the pattern; the vines free
of their luscious burden

filled out the stragglers.
And then I came, just
before pruning,

and walked out in
the morning frost, the sun
clearing the Luberon,

and a thousand droplets,
on a grape cluster,
muscat pavé, told me

that I had a latecomer's
right, to live life out
reflecting, free albeit

tethered, at an angle
to the sun, sweet to you.

Oak Land In Winter

Oaks
are talking
to each other,
by a creek,
saying

from mighty oaks
little acorns
grow.

An
oak
leaf
drift
so thick
it
even
covers
the old
Filets des Maqueraux
can.

A recipe
for a country road:
Plant some oaks
slalom style
between houses.
Let stand
sixty years.
Temperature:
can vary.

The wind
separates
by gravity:
one pile
of acorns,
another
of leaves.

Cold
out-
lines
each
leaf
in
silver;
phase
change,
reunion.

An
acorn
cup
falls
off
as easily as
the
acorn.

The
most
eminently
climbable
crowns
a hill;

its
bark
is
Noah's
ark,
except
the creatures
come
definitely
more
than two by
two.

The
red-green
vine
shows
it's best face
as it begins
a long climb
up bark
to no
good
end.

Their
royal
roundnesses:
At branch end,
a breath-
takingly
symmetrical
ball
of a
gall
with a round
black hole
in,

or
is
it
out
of
it?

Leaves
all
tanned
the color
of calf leather—
the gall
of it.

Dense
oak
shrubs
give
wind
voice.

A fly
lifts off
the ground.
A truffle
oak?

Stunted
by
fungus
but
wanted
alive.

Oh,
colonial
dry land!
Your oaks
harbor
black gold.
And dogs
train
as pilots.

There
are
reasons
to pray
to an oak—
they say
before
one
a dog
will make
you kneel
longer
than
any
priest.

Some
green, live
year round;
some alive,
shedding.
Some holding on
to their leaves
'til spring.
Some letting go.
Like the world,
trying
to have it
all ways.

Buds
will
swell,
buds
push
well.
Buds
can
with ease
do
what
no
wind
will.

Black but Comely

Jessie, the dog really wants
to get under that tree.
So Georges helps, ripping

up the tight branches;
Jessie, after all, does not
deign to look under just

any stunted oak. A genteel
scratch by Jessie, and Georges
is down, digging, and we

all say oo-la-la, for out
of dark-brown earth emerges
this bulbous fist-size growth,

the mother of all truffles.
What shall we say of a black
biomass that wrapped

in two layers of poly-
ethylene, in a day
fills a fridge with the must

turn on semen? We don't dig
black, save oil. We take black
shiny, as hematite and coral,

we are not drawn to grainy
matte black, nor to the brain-
like, but the truffle, untamed

like the black cat I once saw
in a forest, evades factories,
does this inflationary universe

turn on a rhizome thread. Who
needs order out of chaos, when
this taste can come from decay?

The flag of Provence shall be
red like wine, olive green, black
as moonless night, as the truffle.

Birdland

1

A bird is
a bird, is
not
the same bird.

2

To be, a
bird must be
the bird it is:
sparrow, ortolan
warbler, barn owl,
short-toed eagle,
Egyptian vulture,
tit and wren,
magpie.

3

And as it
is seen, it is;
Evert, shaper
of clay birds says,
people, oh
they think a bird
is the same
on both sides.
But it isn't; look
on this side
the feathers are
softly folded back,
there, see, there's
a dangerous
hollow
place.

4
A bird
crossing
fighter
contrails
vouchsafes
flight
in man/bird
heaven.

5
I,
a cedar,
six blackbirds:
the one/many
problem is
nervously re-
solved.

6
A bird
rising; in
the dynamical
correlation
of oak thicket
and cloud, what
was sundered
on the second day
is made
whole.

7
The
scatter
of sparrows
works out
the space
where
they
were.

8

A thrush
sings out, but
it is in a cage, hung
on a tree—no, not
one, but ten! Oh,
how many birds
will make
a *brochette de grives*?
And where, hunter,
will
their breast spots
have gone?

9

One
time,
just one,
a bird, the bird,
dives toward me,
stretches full
into the arrow
that lights up
its target,
the idea
of bird
in me.

The Philosopher's Stone
Found In January

It's a day when the obvious
is incredible; a sunny winter day,
a day to hang the laundry,
for the farmers a day suited
for pruning almonds and cherries,
a day when a walk full of forks
turns into a new great circle,
the mud cakes on my boots, and
between me and life there are
no windows. A boy stacks cut
branches neatly by each tree: red
that was up, red rejoins earth. If
I were an alchemist, I would say
on this day the work is perfected.

IV

Proofs of the Existence of God. I. The Watchmaker Argument

While in the shower, the light goes out and
the house gets awfully quiet. Now, I had
this load of pajamas and filthy socks
in the washer, and, having a Ph.D.
I figure probably the wiring couldn't
take the hot water (the shower was going
for a while, I admit) and the laundry.
So I hie myself to the garage, flip
a few switches, but the one that is red
(15A) stays red. Still the lights go on,
which I take as a good omen, so I re-
start the washer, but five seconds later
everything stops again. I decide that
I'd better finish that wash by hand,
open the front-loading door, whereupon
a load of dark soapy water spills out.
It was time to wash the floor anyway,
and after some mopping I set about
to do just that. But it occurs to me
I might as well bring in wood, which
makes a mess, take that heap of ashes
out. So I fetch the metal basin,
fill it up with ashes, but then there is
near the door this small puddle of water
I somehow missed mopping up, I slip,
do a phantasmagoric save of a
sit-down, holding on to the basin and
without hurting my back. But some ashes
do see their way out, and it happens they
fall mostly into the three pairs of shoes
neatly stacked by the door. I tell myself
that ashes are clean, in the old days folk
even used them to wash. And that today
just might be a very good day to work
on the revision of our paper on
The Rational Design of a Maximal
Electron-Phonon Coupling Constant.

Oligopoem

for Sylvie Coyaud

THEIR PROBLEM
Propylene,
        propylene...
How to relieve
        this boredom
of coupling
        with identical
partners?

SELF CURE
Do froward things:
        twist here, twist
there, the reactive
        end bites...itself,
it happens, in novellas,
        and the ring, well
it says kaput
        to fruitful
propagation.

HUMANS ARE SO UNIMAGINATIVE
A problem? Try
        a second partner!
Each time the live end
        loses its head,
relentlessly
        opting for the other,
stuck in the eternal
        fickleness
of copolymerization.

OURS
On the dizzy chain
        from Sade
to Ziegler, Natta,
        we're into
control; we want
        them strong (or is
it weak?), we want
        Teflon, and epoxy,
all in a day. Lately,
        in a morbid mood,
we've wanted
        the spent ones
to just fall apart.

REPTATION
Polythiophenes,
        anguilles à la Bilbao—
entangled, constricted,
        how else to move
in their crowded Eden?

MONO, OLIGO, POLY
If they could sing
        (I mean beyond
the quantum strum,
        past C-O stretch
and hindered rotation),
        if they could sing
it would be Leadbelly's
        tune; of cousins,
of the hard labor
        of a protein, the
memory of DNA—
        a gang-chained folk,
the utilitarian refrain.

Maya-Spectra

In the Popol Vuh, *the Council Book of the Quiché Maya, Hunahpu and Xbalanque are the conquering and playful twin heroes. And they are players of the Mesoamerican ballgame, in which a rubber ball is hit with a yoke that rides on the hips. The twins are challenged to a lethal ballgame by the twelve lords of Xibalba, the death-dealing rulers of the underworld, whose real names can vanquish them. The twins are up to extracting those secret names...*

The bright beam, sent caroming
off four mirrors of the optical
bench, into the monochromator,

penetrates, invisible but intent; like
the mosquito off on his spying
errand for Hunahpu and Xbalanque,

sly heavenly twins of the Popol
Vuh. For that light means to sting
too, inciting the electron clouds'

harmony with a ball, a wave,
to a state-to-state dance; while
the mosquito flies—in dark rain,

the sun yet unformed—down the Black
Road to Xibalba, bites the false
wooden idols, registering their blank

of an answer, on to the first, who,
god-flesh-bit, cries out, jumps
and the next dark lord calls

"One Death, what is it, One Death?"
which in turn the mosquito records;
from the light is drawn energy,

like blood, leaving on a plotter
a limp signature of H bonded to C;
sampling down the row of heart-

reeking gods: Pus Master, Seven Death,
Bone Scepter, Bloody Claws. The row,
stung, name each other, as do

carbonyl, methyl, aldehyde, amine
prodded by the beam, caught in the end,
like the ball in Xbalanque's yoke.

The losers are sacrificed, the twins win
and life is made clear by signals from within.

Le Chatelier's Principle

The good news on the radio
is that even old people
grow some neurons. Now
prior to that, I confess
I worried a spell about
just doing them in. But
I really shouldn't have,
knowing that deep in
equilibrium is in charge—
things, I mean *your* mo-
lecular things, doing their
razzmatazz thingamajig
in both directions
at the same time. It's
easy to forget, I admit—
the "equi" and the "librium"
both fool you nothing
is happening; it's like
your neighbor at the play,
all of a sudden you
don't hear her breathing
—is she alive, or just
quietly asleep—and you
are faced with a real
decision: oh, experiment
is a tough mistress—
should you pinch her?
Now where was I? Ah yes,
a reproductive biologist, a
Life Peer with a *yarmulka*
told me we lose cells, die
a little, even the first days
after fertilization. So it's
in, at it both ways. And out.

Malacology

for Stephen Jay Gould

All the world
        is in a snail!

Really?

        Well,
                the world's a
        handed in/out
    whirl, matter
through mind.

        You do mean
            the world is
                like a snail's
        shell—*my* snails
    don't whirl!

    You're
        always inter-
                rupting; it's
        in a snail—
    to be slow
or not to be
    slow is not
        the question.
                What is is what
            matter is, how
        it effervesces,
swings.

And mind?

Well, that's wor-
         ry's yen for
                  misaligning
         planetesimals,
making sure
the yarn stays
         tangled and
                  you can't find
                           your teddy bear.

         But a snail—
                  won't it matter
                           it's so glan-
                  dular, all its
biochemistries
on display?

                  That's what I
         said from the
beginning,
         the world is
                  in a snail.

Quantum Mechanics

Beginnings
are always
classical.
It's chemis-
try after
all—to burn
a log needs
to be near
another.

It's at its
most spooky
while growing.
What one may
see, so does
the other;
there being
no evi-
dence entan-
glement falls
off with sep-
aration.

Mature, it
isn't fazed
by singu-
larities,
a theory
that can ac-
comodate
boundary
tensions.

And how will
it end? Like
a love, in
a world de-
monstrably
false, in the
vacuum,
its place filled
by the new.

Of the Land

To enter your landscape
I must reject flatness,
as the sun does burning

off fog in the hills. And
when I have turned the red
sheep of Brazil back into

the termite mounds they are,
I will climb, with vultures,
each valley painting in

the green of another crest.
I will live on berries, yes, I
will fish, and find the way

to reach you, the imaginative
road winding mood-like
in the dust, under trees.

The bamboo thicket sways,
in block clicks. Living on the
landscape we've framed.

Parallel Universes

In Rio de Janeiro no one
is reading Genesis, but
out of the capoeira beat
still a world (or two)
is in formation. In one

I wait for you, and your
coming sure, I leave lights
on, to face my shadow; I
could dance capoeira, oh
I could learn. And in

another world you park
your car, stand, keys
in hand (one shouldn't,
in Rio) and open
the door again. By day,

by night, past pattern
recognition, facts
squirm willfully,
to inform one world
this too makes sense.

Capoeira

I would write to you again,
on the old watermarked

paper. The marks hide, gently
say: this one made me, this

one owns me, this message
does not abandon. Men and

women don't have watermarks,
and they certainly don't like

to be owned by anybody,
or branded deep within. Still

we are marked, by genes, and
remember: the smell of earth

in the bunker, my son's face
when scolded, near to crying;

I hear the capoeira beat.
People say it's important

good memories not be trans-
muted into bad. They say

I have a choice there. I think
it's very important the late snow

remain on the lily of the valley.
That the sun not melt the snow.

That we bend down, together,
to the creamy small bells. That

the snow stay, at least until June.

Planck Was a Good Man

One cool night, Selfishness
pulled the blanket to his side.
Reason felt ire in her letters;
clearly Love had fled the coop.

A century ago, honest Max
Planck followed the black
body radiation law to its in-
eluctable quantum source.

And Einstein's close gander
at light in, an electron out
of a metal, made us all be-
lievers, hypothesis a fact.

Well, I'll tell you this about
that: Planck then spent years
fishing for a way around
the quantum he had wrought.

And Einstein, much appalled
at Danish ways with waves,
out for help in all quarters,
even made God no gambler.

Here, Selfishness, Reason,
and Love huddle daylong
in an astonishingly empty
space, desperate for signs.

Proust and Cézanne

I stand in the midst
of vineyards, whose
time to be cut down
has come. Last year,
I imagine you stood
in the vineyards
of Proust's Combray.
So hard to escape
vineyards in France—
the artful light on
brown rootstocks
in winter, spring's pin-
point grapes, the smell
of spilled juice at
harvest. And a time,
an autumn to winter
time, to prune. A cut,
that will not be re-
membered. Still, this
vineyard makes me
pray, for two, who,
in the end, lived out
their separate dreams
of a France that wears
ruffles of vineyards
over its earth veins.

VI

Fall Follies

I drove my middle-aged car
right over the whirled-up
pile of leaves in Baker court-
yard—that morning I was
coming back from weight-
lifting, feeling in the mood

for exercising free will, there
being plenty of other leaf-free
parking places; I thought, well—
that would make a soft landing
for my Volvo's corroded bottom.
I came back in the afternoon,

and found the leaves under
the car had wended their way
to a more hospitable place
for fallen leaves, and instead, there were quite a few
inside my car. So, I looked

for a rusty hole, big enough
for a leaf to be swirled through;
I mean, I've seen field mice
get into a larder through tiny
cracks, but leaves, who would
imagine such rodent drives

in a mess of yellow heading
into brown? Then a leaf spoke,
said, it wasn't a hole, man,
it usually isn't a hole; it's
you. Open the door, add
some Bernoulli lift, and

while you're grappling
with your gym gear, well,
I admit it, with a little help
from the wind, we just
blow in. Looking around,
I said to myself: beware

when leaves start talking
to you. But, just for insurance,
and speaking to no leaf
in particular—I whispered:
watch it, kid, the leafblowers
are moving through campus.

The Zohar of Aging

When I see you, friend,
mind hog-tied in re-

calcitrant body, you
swatting flies off New

Yorker stacks, your
body asserting hap-

hazard claims to gassy
urgings, you, sick, I

can't help thinking
of the minefield of

God, He dithering past
omniness, mumbling

to Himself (who else
might He talk to?),

through the jury-rigged
construction site, of, oh

give them hell, the pre-
Big-Bang universe. And

like you, shuffling to
the world's overstuffed

medicine cabinet, He
also had to look for

His glasses (while a galaxy
or two spun off His

stumbling), and He too
put them down smack dab

into the vaseline jar the
tempter nudged right there,

and both of you, in the
ache, curse, and axing act

of survival, tease out
word, the world, a song

that came before song,
ground truths, this:

the beginning (after
the end that will
not come) created God.

We Will Not Be Moved

Tired, as tired as museums
can make them, or waiters'
hundred dollar in tips
seven-hour night shifts, heel
twisted in grate, flat, fallen
flat, swollen after a New
York–Tokyo non-stop, unused
to high clogs in Yoshino,
size 6½ or 35, metatarsals
sore, recalling hopscotch,
sticky oats, black sand under-
foot, ingrown toenails, yet
I could have danced all night
cumbia, merengue, alligator-
boot shod, Reebok sneaker sore,
hot for air, socks off,
oh—long soaking, the pumice
stone's soft scrape, fingers, her
kneading, licked as in a book
or by cat, up and at them
again, blisters Band-Aided,
stepping on, up, off, into
space, to a jig, in dog do,
the wine gone to my feet feet.

Polheim, Dec. 17, 1911

...the date Roald Amundsen reached the South Pole.
And the name he gave his camp....

In the lone place
where a man could

stand and track
his shadow's near

circle in the snow,
Amundsen frets

(of cologned scoffers),
and so they stay

another day, shoot
the sun in six-

hour shifts; Amundsen
dreams in his furs,

of black men huddled
like sheep on a rock,

the moon there, in
the Antarctic

night, diamonds strung
in the sky. There's

no sextant to tell
these men where they

are; one who looks
like his father,

tears a burning
branch from the fire

(the moon dances
in the heat) and

the man, smiling
in his small power,

throws the torch
to the sky where

a trail of sparks
pierces stars, in

the sound one's breath
makes in the arctic

as ice crystals form
and fall. Amundsen

wakes, it is time
to plant a flag,

stun and slaughter
the uncommonly good-

natured Helge,
who is portioned

to the sixteen
other dogs. They leave

Helge's teeth, and
the tuft at the

end of his tail
for the next man

to reach Polheim.

Ground Truths

My teachers said:
a good builder
needs six things:
water, clay, timber,
stones, canes, and iron;
if not canes, surely
a measuring rod.

I did them right,
learned the trade,
to adobe added
an orbital world
or two. A good boy,
I threw no shadow
across their equation.

Until one day questions
beset me—why build,
whose abode, why some
strut when others kneel?
They said: ah, ah, silly
boy—we don't ask,
we're just builders.

I said, things take
rod-sure shape—fly-
overs, rap, Hockney's
photomontages,
helices that turn left
then right, even key lime
pie, my God that's new!

They said, nothing
the sun hasn't seen,
kid—bend down. So

I bent, low, saw
Douglas fir needles,
a shaft of light, and
oh, the chanterelle.

This-and-No-Other-ness

sticks white
to grass
dusted by
a sunrise
squall out-
of-season,
elm trunks'
snow shadows

elsewhere
the wind
rustles left
corn, cobs
half-eaten,
the stalks
straggling
gray uphill
in shale-
spattered
Carlisle
ground.

They found
the Bismarck
a mile down,
its 15-foot
swastika
peeling, a ring
of pairs of
unpalatable
boots poking
through the
placid sea-
bottom sand.

From Surfeit to Dearth

things, just
out there or
in,
seem to beg to be
    arranged in formation. So thought to be described,
        are in fact in formation—fine,
      but what matters spiritually for things
        is *in* formation,
          after which they return
to being
things

VII

Interface

From a "please yourself" or
the freeze in a hug, an edge

grows. Maelstrom love
to one side, you might think,

coexistence to the other. But
as we drive along, the edge

is like the mountains in
Civil War colors shifting

behind August corn, like
the dislocation under a

tunneling microscope, order
well disposed to each side.

Only the edge is defined. It
moved when I looked back.

Homecoming

The day the war ended
we came home to Ithaca

found our children safe,
toys still in the closet. So

we put them to sleep, in
rooms crammed with old

clothes, dishes, the debris
of whoever lived here.

In the middle of the night
I awoke, and thought—what

if other children hid here,
during the war, wandered

in, hid by themselves,
in the closets, in the attic.

And then, what if the night
divided against them, and

they, in their sad skins, in
the cold, or locked in…. We

must look for them. So
I woke you, you understood

and quietly, kerosene lamps
in hand, we walked together
the crowded rooms of our house.

Fields of Vision

From the attic the boy
watched children playing, but

they were always running
out of the window frame.

And the weathered shutters
divided up space, so

that he couldn't often tell
where the ball Igor kicked

(he heard the children call
Igor's name) would end up.

The boy was always moving,
one slat to another,

trying to make the world
come out. He saw Teacher

Dyuk's wife with a basket,
then he saw her come back

with eggs; he could smell them.
Once he saw a fat goose,

escaped from her pen, saved
from slaughter, he thought. Once

he saw a girl, in her
embroidered Carpathian

vest. He couldn't see the sky,
the slats pointed down; he

saw the field by the school,
always the same field, only

snow turned into mud into
grass into snow. Later

the boy grew up, came
to America, where he

was a good student, praised
for his attention to facts;

he taught people to look
at every distortion

of a molecule, why
ethylene on iron

turned this way, not another.
In this world, he thought, there

must be reasons. His poems
were not dreamy, but full

of exasperating
facts. Still later, he watched

his mother, whose eyes were
failing, move her head, the

the way he did, to catch
oh a glimpse, the smallest

reflecting shard of light
of our world, confined.

Communication Problems

They needed each other,
and as I wonder why, I
imagine he too tried

to understand what had
come of the stray seed
set in a murky tide pool.

A time he spoke to them,
like one man to another;
a few heard, the others

ignored him. So he hid
his voice in whirlwinds,
and then, thinking they'd

listen closer to their own,
spoke through prophets.
When this didn't work

he tried dreams. Oh, they
were in want of guidance,
these people; even wise kings

had to be told not to go
to Herod, and the next
moment, Joseph to take

his small family to Egypt.
Still later he resorted
to planting visions, in

Theresa and Hildegard.
Now he despairs, dreams
gone to angst, churches

in control of visions. He
sends signs, but these grown
quiet—the sway of a stalk

where a grasshopper sat,
the tree snail shells, rain
still needed for a rainbow.

The Golden Boxes of Forgetting

A large room was built
for the ceremony; we

enter, to forget, put an
end to, forget. Each

brings a golden box,
you do, and I. Some carry

two or three. In each box
a scroll, a memory

written in Serbian, or
Yiddish, in Armenian,

Turkish, Chinese, Hutu,
Croatian, and Ukrainian.

For this we prepared
a year, writing each day

until no more could be
written, writing more

the next day. We stack
the boxes in the center

of the room, where fire
comes; we sit and watch

them burn, burn all night.
All around the world,

for six days, people burn
the gilt boxes of forgetting.

2

On Mauna Kea, on
the big island

of Hawaii, the lava
flows are labeled

by neat brown signs.
Pele's '97 act still

has a whiff of sulfur
dioxide; '94's black

cinders cut my shoes,
but after six years,

there are flowers, in
fifty only fertile earth.

3

Fifty-six years ago they
killed you, father. How

shall I fill my golden
box of forgetting, when

I could not, at five,
nestle into your arms?

Enough Already

You walk in to the sun-
splashed olives' mossy

trunks, greener than
fresh grass. This doesn't

seem to be enough
so you think—even

here they grow olives
only on warm terraces;

and ask who first found
olives had to be cured?

This cleverness, too
does not satisfy. So,

walking hand-in-hand
into the grove you say:

the world needs us
(and other lovers)

to give such life; which
would do nicely for most,

save those who'd leave it
for a Creator. But

then, alone, you look
real close, and the black

spot on the green bark
you reach for sharpens

into inch-and-a-half of
scorpion, you see a

red beetle, and by God,
that does suffice.

About the Author

Roald Hoffmann's fourth poetry collection explores the beautiful and terrible world around and within us. He was born in Złoczôw, Poland in 1937, survived the Nazi occupation, and moved to the U.S. where he graduated from Columbia University and received his Ph.D. from Harvard University. Since 1965 he has taught at Cornell University, where he is now the Frank H. T. Rhodes Professor of Humane Letters and Professor of Chemistry. He has received numerous honors including the Nobel Prize in Chemistry in 1981.

Roald Hoffmann has previously published three poetry books, *The Metamict State*, *Gaps and Verges*, and his most recent collection, *Memory Effects*.